Lineberger Memorial
Library

MOST ANCIENT
OF ALL
SPLENDORS

Johann Moser

MOST ANCIENT
OF ALL
SPLENDORS

SOPHIA INSTITUTE PRESS
Manchester, New Hampshire

Library of Congress Cataloging-in-Publication Data
Moser, Johann M., 1940-
    Most ancient of all splendors / by
    Johann M. Moser.
    ISBN 0-918477-07-7 Cloth
    I. Title.
PR3563.08839M6 1989   811'.54 – dc19   88-34644   CIP

✝

August Wilhelm Moser

München: August 16, 1914

Innsbruck: September 9, 1957

IN PATRIS MATRISQUE MEMORIAM

Elizabeth Schrafft Moser

Newton, MA: January 29, 1915

Laconia, NH: July 25, 1988

✝

The Poems

MOST ANCIENT
OF ALL
SPLENDORS

The Larks of Umbria

Can vei la lauzeta mover
de joi sas alas contral rai
que s'oblid' es laissa chazer
per la doussor c'al cor li vai....

Bernart de Ventadorn

The larks,
   Always the larks...
      Above the valleys
And the mountains,
    Pale-green as celery in the spring;
Water-lilies
     Below the ancient bridge,
   Red poppies by the wayside —
      When I sang alone
Amid the chestnut forests,
     Walking those primaeval roads,
Restoring the stone-girt walls
   Of old San Damiano close by Assisi.
Friends came;
    Friends followed me through sunny days,
Heralds of the morning,
      Jongleurs of the Hidden King,

Dancing in the freshness of new-born light.
We slept under hedges.
     We besought the lame and scornful.
Like campaniles of the towns,
   We rang out our gentle benison over all the earth:
Birds, flowers, the woodland game,
     Blushed as in "early love" of Eternity.
But soon the thronged processions
     Winding down to Portiuncula!
The brotherhood, the crowds,
     Hilarious and desolate,
  Besotted with sullied ikons of human sanctity!
I fled into the mountains —
    My sole auberge, a hut of reeds;
Brother Wolf, my Brother Falcon,
     Sole companions of those darksome hours;
And cold winds from the western sea
  Rushed through bleak cols of snow-clad peaks.
Then, over Monte La Verna,
      (ô Monte la Verna!)
  Dawn upon sheer dawn,
    Splendor upon sheer splendor,
Bordure of the heavens flaming-red
    And turreted wings rasping high above me —
The unfathomable Seraphic Wasp,
  Scorching blood-wounds in my hands and feet,
Luminous,
   Suffering,
     Beloved beyond all measure.
I came once more into the lowlands,
    Once more among the peopled ways:

The cities on the hills,
    The olive groves, the fields of grain.
I consoled; I was consoled.
        I judged no longer. And now I wait.
I braid the hempen cord of earthly days;
    I bend my blinded eyes towards the sun.
And I listen:
        The larks,
            Always the larks...
        Caroling through the deep-blue skies
            In joyous antiphons of praise.

Berceuse

Aged rafters bend and sigh
    Beneath the frosty hush of winter.
Cinnamon and chestnuts,
   Apples, wheels of cheddar cheese,
Repose within the larder.
     The latchkey has been turned.
An earthen-crock of warm molasses,
   The kneaded bread beside the hearth,
Lend fragrance to the midnight hour.
     The household sleeps.
I wedge a block of knarry wood
      into the flames;
Sparks brighten the darkness.
    Ruddy frets of firelight
Burnish an old brass ewer,
  A pewter pot and ladle in the corner.
On the gnarled-oak bedstead,
    The eiderdown stirs softly.
I reflect upon the heft of seasons,
   Voices in long twilights by the fire,
Infants bedded down, then,
   Like seeds in the warm, fertile earth.

They sleep soundly.
    I would have them prosper…
        …ripen into the fullness of all things:
The lantern shall burn late tonight;
    A blackened inkhorn rests upon the table.
Outside the cabin windows
    Spruce boughs shimmer in the icy moonlight.
Reindeer herds are moving now
        Over silent tundra and arctic forests.
And dark-cloven fiords,
            snowy spurs of wintry oceans,
Slumber in the starlit robe of night.

Wyoming Rain

Over studded mountains,
  High-timbered slopes of the Absaroka,
Hear:
  Storms of summer, swarthy-throated,
      thundering down into the valleys.
Hayfields buckle,
    Dust whirls on sagebrush hills,
Lightning brindles blackened skies.
And rain:
  Rain over grassy tablelands and wooded hollows,
Over white-bouldered rivers
    and bottomlands of cottonwood and aspen;
Slender sheaves of rain —
      Purple, gold, across the wilderness,
Trailing to bronze-rimmed prairies eastward.
And now,
  The glittering pinnacles of cloud and sun;
Glad arroyos splash,
      dazzle amid canyons.
Sunlight showers
    through tender-dripping forests

And wet bark of giant spruce,
              ponderosa —
Fragrant in the valley winds.
Among clusters of gooseberry leaves,
   A black bear shrugs his dusky hide;
A puma sniffs the clear, cool air.
And listen:
   Birds are singing in the mountains.

Lochland: A Memoir

(Squam Lake, N.H.)

Lichened rocks,
    Blue-green seams of shore and cove,
Red squirrels among the juniper,
  And lucent days
      as quiet as raspberries in the sun —
Those silences, Lochland —
       land of lake and forest,
"Lake of the shining peace" —
     Those silences you imparted....
For I recall that low-eaved lodge
       beneath the hemlocks:
Logs sparkling in the stony hearth
  When the lake was cold and gray,
And wood-smoke curled upwards
    through the damp forest.
I have thought of white-cuffed waves
  Glittering in blue gusts from the mountains,
Sailboats yawing
    towards the Holderness Narrows,

And lean-bouldered hills, glacier scarred,
  Knuckled to the braided winds
        of distant polar seas.
And I remember the call of loons
        over the evening lake,
The aroma of pine in the cool night,
    And moon cusped low above wooded islands —
Nocturnal eyes,
    Nocturnal ears, bent to the stillness:
A stir of leaves in the forest,
        A ripple of starry galaxies
Upon the lull of waters.
    Those silences, Lochland,
        Those silences you imparted....

Old Gander's Weeping

Spring melt-back,
  Maples in red bud,
April woods
  Still sharp as winter in the notches,
Mud on fields and sunny snow —
  That's when we buried her
Down at Burrow's Corner.
  Her folks from Wonalancet came to help;
Anyhow, we got the sugarin' done.
  Barn needs mending, too, 'fore autumn.
'Ought to buck the pine behind the saphouse —
  It fell last January in the storm.
Pine's not like oak, not like ash:
  Pine won't bear grief.
I still can see her, though,
  On the high-deck of that old paddle-wheeler,
Steaming its way up Winnipesaukee.
  She saw me; we got married.
She came like she went:
  Pert, and hale, and sudden,
As a hummingbird in a woodland clearing.
  She liked Christmas best of all:

Corn-roasts, dancing at the grange,
   Sledding on the frosty hills
About the verge of evening.
   But the birds are sad this summer.
No raking blueberries either;
   They tumble, ungathered, to the ground.
The flowers wilt among the ragweed.
   No herbs hang from the rafters of the porch.
At high-mowing,
   She'd bring the rig up from the valley,
Fetching fresh johnnycake and cider —
   The boys loved that, resting by the brook.
I was so proud:
   She had more living in her
Than fifty acres put to corn.
   Someday I'd bring my rig down, too,
Down to Burrow's Corner.
   I think she needs me now.
The nights grow colder.
   We'd sleep together as we did,
Beneath the lid of earthen days,
   Beneath the winter moon.

Floridean Ragas

1

Dawn —
    Moist conch of night,
Espalier of stars
          sloping westwards.
Watermelon bloom
      at bounds of ocean;
Earth, copper-green;
    Dark-shadowed roses in the south wind,
And sun,
    Huge and brassy,
Yawning by the banlieus of the sea.

2

White ships
      in breezy estuaries;
White banners
      Fluttering among the docks;
The sun-bleached piers
          and pelicans asleep

In the lucid morning light.
        Beyond surf-spray
The avocado beaches,
    Coquina shanties overshadowed
By palm trees
        gusting in the wind;
And clouds like sunny caravels
    Sail the blue horizons of the sea.

3

Bones of old estancias,
    Sea-walls crumble into surf;
The broad sea-rust;
    And saw-leaved savannahs
Blazing in the heat.
    The sun, as musty and as wan
As the way I travel.
        Inland, the orange-groved hills;
Southland forest hung with moss;
    Dim shadows bending with the breeze;
And all those gentle hues
        of noontide ease.

4

The sun has vanished
        in resplendent fire —
A gush of rain
        over swampy forests,
Over the glades.

Then, from the weary
Water-laden earth:
    The songs of crickets,
A cool, twilight wind,
      And dragonflies
Hunting in the mangrove —
    While night awakens from the sea,
Shuffling dusky locks
      and drowsy head.

5

Tides in starlight;
    Webbed plains, now,
And palmy islands
  Beneath an ascending moon.
Ocean winds
    upon the cool-slumbering earth
And night-blooming jasmine,
      alluring, aromatic,
Curling slender limbs
        around the stars.

Return to East Pepperell

He bringeth forth his fruit in his season.

Psalm 1

The village lights gleam faintly through the snow
  This winter's evening; Advent glimmers in the windows
Of gaunt, old houses that shelter me as I walk by;
  And the wind is harsh and cold along the street —
"A boisterous wind, hard out of Thrace."
  I remember these same snowy lanes in twilight
When, late for choir, I scudded through the icy drifts
  With some Palestrinean "Gloria" resplendent in my head.
The nights were ablaze with Christmas pageantry,
  With candied fruit and crimson flowers, song and gilded prayer.
Old Monseignor Reilly marshalled all these earthly ways,
  His eyes alit with Paradise; and like an Aran farmer
Stooped with tenderness and age, he nurtured in stony soil
  Our sparse and fragile sprigs of ancient learning.
The harvest of that learning was my life;
  And I left East Pepperell so many years ago.
At college I set sail among the seas of wisdom:
  For we steeped ourselves in antique tongues,

We trod the cloistered ages clad in *philosophia perennis*,
 And our "dumb-ox" out of Sicily shook the timbers of the world.
Later with the Jesuits down on Fillmore Street,
 I knew the sound of schoolyards, of scuffling feet and pens,
Of fledglings battened in a jubilee of mind.
 Those were proud days, then — days of joyous reckoning:
We collected for the missions, observed the great novenas;
 We festooned St. Patrick's Feast with daffodils and clover,
Rallying at Jamie's Tavern before the grand parade.
 The crowd from St. Margaret's came up one year
And we picnicked on the beach at Gloucester,
 Partaking of the bright sun and ivory-tasseled sea.
Then those clamorous football meets at Holy Cross! —
 When flailing in the stands like angry cherubim,
We embraced the autumn sky with cheers and laughter
 While chants of ancient clansmen hovered in the air.
But how shall I recount all that glorious entourage
 Of times and seasons, brimming like the waters of life itself
Tilted yet so high in our bold Hibernian cups?
 Year on year we wrestled with those sinewy Attic voices,
Warming a winter's afternoon with choroi from *The Frogs*
 Or declaiming with hollow Oedipean eyes,
"Ho kakà kakà telôn...": the ineluctable surd.
 For the streets of Boston grew stale with cankered fruit
And our best had perished in the fullness of its days.
 Among those aged wards and clapboard alleyways
Does Aristophanes still jangle in their dreams?
 I do not know. Again I walk these old familiar lanes
Of East Pepperell. The whirling snow gladdens my heart.

I muse the mysterious concourse of the years:
The beginning, the end, and all that came between —
"The shadowy mountains and the echoing sea."

You have fructified me, Lord of Worlds.
*   You have entwined my days like laurel leaves*
To grace the proud, loquacious dead.
*   For my feet have danced in the measure of their dances*
And my lips have sung in the measure of their songs.
*   And now with laurel leaves You bind*
The golden circlet of my life —
*   That crowned with kindly death I wake*
To bestride the wings of chariots
*   And mount in festal splendor to the stars.*

Notker's Last Confession

Monastery of St. Gall
Switzerland, 912 A.D.

No, it was not befitting...
   ...That season of the year, that journey
Upon some minor point
          of discipline or land:
The ways long and arduous,
   Valleys frozen beyond St. Gall,
Ice-bound rivers, lakes,
   Villages smouldering in the frosty air
And flagons of hot wine
   Gulped beside the fires of lonely, upland farms.
When, towards early evening,
   In a golden winter forest,
Suddenly...a wolf!
   A wolf beneath the hedgethorn!
I struck,
   Cowl flung back, rush of woollen sleeves,
Staff raised high...
   ...and blood-stained snow.
No harm had been meant,
   I saw...too late.
Glad springtime came
   And all the festal sequences of days and years:

Bright summers,
  Somber winters gathered to the praise
Of peace and holiness.
  And now I stand at the brim of deep eternity,
Berueing only...
  The haste...the fear...the faithlessness
Before those gentle,
  Before those kindly
Perils...
  ...of my life;
And the dying wolf —
  Felled among those snowy mountains.
  ....Forgive me this.

Epistle unto Asaph,
Guardian of the King's Forest

Amen dico tibi, hodie mecum eris in Paradiso.
Luke 23:43

In Paradiso, et "in Paradiso."
Unto my Lord and Servant, Asaph, say —
Thus, the Great King, highest among Thrones,
Lord of Lords, and Prince of Dominions:
Peace. And in thy ample courts,
Coolness of summer days and sweet repose.
He bids thee, Asaph, bind the scattered leas
Of This, His Royal Park and Sanctuary,
And set the boundaries of His Lands in order.
He bids thee span the contours of the wilderness
And gather all things, according to their kinds,
That Like to Like, and Unlike to Unlike, shall adorn
This most Ancient of all Splendors of His Days.
Then spread the high plateaus with lean-grain grasses
And fashion reedy margins by the streams,
Where tamarisk and willow may share the scented breeze.
Endow the flowering woodlands with paths and fountains
And mossy archways, rock-hewn balustrades
Winding down to leafy grottos in the shade.
Plant groves of lime and orange on the sunny hills

[23]

And many-towered vineyards plant there, too,
Heady with the musk of deep-slumbering wine.
Replenish all His sacred ground with living creatures:
With zebras, dromedaries, with highland pandas,
And bright flamingos basking by the rim of pallid seas.
Give shape to that which would be shaped;
Let be whatever shapes itself most graciously:
The sleepy bayous, dozing in the midday sun,
And slender-fluted forests, thronged with birds,
With tulips lush and wild amidst the fragrant loam.
Let be the hush of tawny plains and island lakes
And rose-drooped cliffs like crimson cataracts,
Dazzling, joyous, beneath the pale-blue sky.
And tender unto each and every thing
Its own dear, inimitable Self:
That they may be, as all in all,
One Living Song among His Eternal Mountains.
Then gird it round with Gates of Love
And bow thy head, and seek thy rest,
For I, His Envoy, vouchsafe to thee
This very day thou dwellest with Me
In Paradiso, et "in Paradiso."

Momentary Reprieve at Konotop
(The Ukraine, 1943)

Kak horosho, i kak priytno zheet bratym vmesste.
Psalm 132

Battle's final rancor; and then, the stillness.
    Blistered plains fumed beneath the darkened skies.
Through rising gusts we scanned the dreadful sedge of combat:
    Scuttled tanks, half-tracks tipped and burning on the roads,
Embankments strewn with helmets, boots, and shattered gear
    And all that weary cargo, weary cargo, of the dead.
We buried them, ours and theirs. They, too, among us,
    Bent their spades to the unripened harvest and the bitter soil.
And the rain began: sparse, cold globules of rain,
    Clotting the heat, the dust, the anguish of parched hands
And blackened mouths, and bodies soured by filth and sweat.
    The winds rose up; the vessels of the sky were broken.
Thick spasms of rain throbbed and thundered over the land.
    Hot machine guns spumed and hissed; trucks steamed.
And we ran for cover, crowding under tarpaulins and oilskins,
    With shredded apparel, gray-green and violet-brown,
Tangled in heaps of bandages, of soiled flesh, and mud.
    Then we huddled together, chattering and trembling.

We jeered at grimy faces and blood-stained rags;
  We grinned at bashful jokes muttered in alien tongues;
And we broke bread together — bread, dank and black —
  Sharing the fragile sustenance, yes, "all the amenities":
Sausage, beans, the pungent haze of Machorka tobacco,
  Coffee brewed in rusty cans and laced with vodka.
We sang, too, thumping out some Armenian song
  None of us understood. We sang and railed and laughed,
Laughed at the uproarious, heedless rain, the blessed rain,
  That asperged all we had seen — all we were yet to see.
Later the storm abated; rain fell gently over the earth.
  Under sodden coverlets we lay: still, forgetful,
With bodies knotted, heads bent, to the hard repose.
  The rain stopped; horizons of the evening cleared.
Silent armies slept in the cool breath of the steppes.
  The sun, deep-red, blood-red, like a bullet wound,
Slooped backwards into the immense shroud of night;
  And all those pallid, shivering stars leaned down,
Forsaking their sad vigilance, to slumber by our sides.

Bordeaux, 408 A.D.

(in two voices)

"At anchor in the harbor, now,
   Galleys of the western fleet prepare to sail.
The sun rides low beyond the ocean;
   On our table, a cruet of Burdigalan wine
Glows fiery-red in evening light,
   And we watch the somber nightfall
      Lean its brow upon the sea."

"Should we not prepare to leave as well?"

      "Where would we go?
The Augustan legions are withdrawn;
    The Rhine frontier has fallen.
Like bats in a gutted tower,
    The *foederati* flutter through the empire
Seeking a blackened perch amid the ruins.
    And Alaric turns his raven's eye
Down the Flaminian viaducts,
   Down to the Alban Hills, and — dare I say it? —
'The walls of lofty Rome.'
    The stays of the imperium cannot hold."

"But the matter of perpetuity!"

"Ah, we can but cherish what has been bestowed;
We can but praise what lived before us,
    And will yield its gracious foison to the ages.
Perpetuity renders us,
        But is not ours to render; all human excellence
Alone is quarried in the hands of God.
            But look, upon the darkening waves,
The galleys trim their starboard lamps."

            "When will they depart?"

"They sail with the tide, those ships;
            They will not come again.
Lucinius has joined them.
        He stuffed his earthen jars with scraps:
Souvenirs of the old campaigns —
    A battered eagle or two, medallions from Trier.
What does it matter? He sails for Spain.
        The *barbaroi* will be there to meet him.
Shall he embark for Africa?
    Numidian grain-fields shall be red with blood
Before he unpacks his wares."

        "And us?"

                "...compose the hymns
Which they at morning will intone
        To laud the new-born sun, the ancient land,

The same ripened apples
        Loaded into carts at harvest-time.
Someday they too shall walk these hills
        And take the poplars for their song
And sing a lady's beauty.
        Someday they too shall aptly raise
Basilicas of thought into the heavens."

        "Until then...?"

"Until then...?
        The wine, my friend, a final cup;
The night is growing heavy,
        And I must homeward bend my way
To stave my lids, my weary soul,
        Against that long-encroaching,
                That dark and ageless sea.
May Roman peace betide us
        Among the solemn groves,
The sepulchres of our fathers in their sleep."

Testament of Sheba

*The Queen of the South shall rise up...for she came from
the ends of the earth to hear the wisdom of Solomon....*
Matthew 12:42

Eastward, over windy moorlands,
      The sun like a waking lion,
The herdsman's lance,
      And long-winged shadows, fleeting backwards,
Seek roost upon that Solitary Tree
      At the far edge of this World —
When we hoist saddles, mats, the worsted awnings,
      Nursing waterskins at rills from melted snows
High beyond the Harra plateau.
  And we lead our camels downwards, through dark defiles,
To the salt-sinks and great flint-plains
      Of the western desert.
Above us, in languorous wheels,
    Hawks and buzzards veer in the limpid morning sky.
Day-heat burgeons swiftly:
      Parched wadis, glassy crusts of pumice-beds,
Glazed-blue shards of mountains
      Glimmer along the low horizon,
As we ply these burnt and hallowed lands,

Bearing upon our litters the scarce inheritance —
No provender but locusts
        Cured and toasted, packed in leather pouches,
Ashy flat-bread, citron rinds —
        A narrow sustenance so humbly, so princely, cherished.
"No humankind shall find salvation,
                Unless he shall endanger himself."
On a distant rise, a cheetah lopes softly
        Through the hot blades of the desert wind.
High-churning pillars of dust
    Pass to southward; silent dunes undulate around us,
While camels' flaggy lips beseech
        Endurance in the seasons of their affliction.
We arrive, in evening, at a fruitful valley:
        A valley of date-palms and wild peppermint
And flowering acacia,
        Redolent with honey-bees and yellow desert blossoms.
Here, the wizened udders of the soil
        Seep forth freshets of cool, spring water.
Here, like turbaned kings of old,
                We invoke in adoration
Lord Jêsa, son of Miriam, Massiah,
    Blessed over all the earth, unceasing to be blessed,
Bespoken of Gabriel,
        Bespoken of forty-thousand prophets in days of awe.
Shall not, through Him, the very stones be raised
                Children unto Ibrahim our Father?
We enkindle, then, the sweet broom-fire;
        The rebeck mourns a wilderness
As black and lustrous as sheer obsidian;
        Tethered camels sleep.

And God rides His green-bright Dolphin
    Through planetary seas and astral oceans.
Lizards lift moon-cratered eyes;
    Cicadas sing.
Tabernacles of the stars
    Whirl in ancient ecstasy across the night.

The Neighing of Kourkig Jelaly

It is said that on every Friday
Water drips from the rock.
That water, they say, drips from Kourkig Jelaly;
And travelers passing by the rock on Fridays
Hear the neighing of Kourkig Jelaly.

Old Armenian *David of Sassoun*

And on that final day
    The mountainous barbican of Akravou Kar
Shall be cleft asunder;
    And the Horn shall shake the barren highlands,
The wind-lashed Lake of Van;
        And buffalos shall scatter
Among the chenar trees —
        For Thou, Kourkig Jelaly,
    Lightning Steed,
        Steed of Justice,
Rearest forth,
        Caparisoned in glory,
With falcon-eyes and fiery mane
        Bounding towards the resplendent skies!
And the shudder of Thy nostrils

Shall be dreadful over the nations,
The skirr and din of harness,
    The clangor of golden spurs above the clouds!
And in the tempest of Thy stride
        The brittle world shall be transformed:
Wheat shall bloom like roses,
    Barley like the walnut trees,
Black loam of earth —
        Firm, abundant, blossoming
Under the clatter of thunderous hoofs;
        And seas like pomegranate wine,
Orange-red, incarnadine;
    Jasper mountains gleaming in the sun!
"And I saw a White Horse
        Posted at the Paddocks of Heaven."
Kourkig Jelaly,
    Lightning Steed, Steed of Justice;
Kourkig Jelaly,
    Steed of Love, Steed of Life,
        Galloping through alabaster worlds
And panoplies of agate stars,
        Bearing the reborn shrags of time
Upwards into the dazzling Night,
    Upwards into the pastures of Eternity!

Alisaunder of Macedoine

e'l gran centauro disse: 'E'son tiranni
che dier nel sangue e ne l'aver di piglio.
Quivi si piangon li spietati danni;
quivi e Alessandro....'
                    Inferno, XII, 104-7.

For the lodestar flashed in the deep blue night...
                ...the diamantine lure, lure of dominion.
And we came to a land abounding in lions,
        A land of pyramids and peacock wings;
And we spread devastation around us,
        Hauling away the spoils of conquest
                    Into the fronded hills of the east.
We traversed mountain fastnesses
        Where woolly onagers clambered on rocky steeps,
Watching us as we passed.
    We knew the dread hoar-frost, the trek through blizzards,
Encampments in valleys benumbed with ice,
        And snowy plains melting beneath the sun.
We descended into arid country
                    Beyond the great-forked rivers
And saw herds of six-legged men there

[35]

Scrambling like spiders over the desert.
And some of us wanted to turn back then,
   But we left their entrails reeking on the torrid sands.
Later, in regions of mist and rain,
      A host of spiky crustaceans
            Arose from the pluvious fenlands;
And we mounted battle in that place,
            Swinging massy fire-pots and torches,
Driving them back into the lurid waters.
         Then we entered a wilderness of thorns
Where partridges, snarling, dog-headed,
   Gripped our swollen shanks. But we shook them off and fled
When a golden-tusked oryx
      Bellowed at us from a forest of reeds.
We came at last to the broad littorals of the earth:
   Dracontine headlands, slumbering in the ocean swells,
Where ancient dhows with lateen sails
   Luffed windward in the soft salt-breeze,
And dugongs, perched on coral cliffs,
   Laughed at us and plunged into the sunlit seas.
And, at the furthest capes of land,
      Amid heaps of tarnished arms and dusty trophies,
We perished in our fright:
         For the sun seeped from golden urns
Through blackest clouds and topaz planets,
   Skeletal foxes barked at the death-mask of the moon,
And antlered gods in shawls of fire
      Danced upon the mountains.
For the lodestar flashed in the deep blue night...
      ...the diamantine lure, lure of dominion.

Admiral of the Ocean-Sea

Jesus cum Maria
Sit nobis in via.

"They shall give glory to the Lord,
    And declare His praise among the many Islands."
For all had been bespoken thus,
        thus ordained:
  The ancient books, the charts, Ser Marco Polo,
Those old Arab navigators,
    Ghosting the rim of the *mare tenebrosum* —
"The Green Sea of Gloom,"
  Looped with sea-worms, gusty regents of the winds,
And visions of the far Antilles.
          I remembered Dom Henrique,
His lonely outpost on the western headlands,
    And spice fleets fresh in from Malagueta,
Riding high at the quays of Lisbon.
    And, ever before me, beckoning,
          demanding,
That full, uncharted quadrant of the Ocean-Sea.
    "When thou shalt pass over the Mighty Waters,
I shall be with thee."
    The bannerols of discovery were unfurled;

the pendants fluttered.
The Purple Lions of Aragon,
          The Golden Turrets of Castile,
Mounted on our boisterous mastheads,
     We dipped before a fair land-breeze,
Skirting the pine-clad dunes
               and marshy promontories,
Where, from the chantry of La Rabida,
     We could hear: *"Jam lucis orto sidere."*
The hour was prime;
  The Rio Saltes yawned and stretched.
Beyond sand-bars...
     ...Blue water! Blue water!...
               the yard arms laughing
And yare hulls hove into the kindly sea.
     Buffeting to the headwinds, then,
               sheer off the Sagres Roads
We dropped astern the sacred soil of Europe.
          The Ocean-Sea bulged high before us
Like the hump of a sleepy camel
     Laden with dreams of golden cities,
Of mint-eyed girls and airy palaces
          Close under an oriental moon.
Beyond the Canary Calms we traced
     The arc of the western azimuth,
Sailing into brilliant sunsets,
     And strange constellations in the night.
We savored the plash of days on days —
          Pelagic birds skimmed overhead,
               dolphins rode the vessels' wash,

And mornings were the spring in Andalusia
    When the Guadalquivir swirls softly past
          the towered gardens of Seville.
We encompassed, too, the squalls of men and timbers:
    The thrash of halyards,
        Braying throats and shredding spars,
Prayers, regrets, imprecations,
    And, amid the fury, a voice as sweet
        as heaven's sternward cresset —
"Tierra! Tierra!"
   Before our eyes, dawn-bedecked sierras
      Broke like sorrel stallions from the sea!
For how should I, Colombo, mariner,
    Christo-ferens, have summoned the earth
To this most glorious enterprise? —
      Cordilleras wood-begirt, the verdant cays,
Palmy coves and harbors,
    Brushed by the turquoise eyelids of the sea,
And flocks of bright-hued parrots
   Like rose petals,
     whirling, showering against the sun.
I thought I had found Paradise.
     But in bearing Christ, I bore the Cross as well.
O blood of Hispaniola!
  O blood of the slaughtered caciques, upon my hands!
And the shoals of the Golden Chersonese,
     Awash in lust and terror and remorse!
May the high plains of the windy Estramadura,
   The Virgin's lean hands and sorrowful countenance,
Cover my shame in dust

And vindicate my honor before the nations.
May my city, *Genova la Superba*,
        Find ever consolation in my name,
    "Because from it I came, and in it I was born,"
Who, braced in the boundless arms of God,
        Brought the *lumen fidei* to the Indies
And worked His wonders upon the Ocean-Sea.

The Necropolis at Cerveteri

Pink-speared asphodels are blooming once again
    Among the tufa-stones
        and old escarpments of the city:
A stark sun-bitten landscape,
    The sough of sea-wind in the tall arbutus...
As we descend,
    Like ancient flamens bearing torches,
Into the grassy tumuli
        And dank, heady humors of the earth.
Our lanterns sever the darkness.
    Terracotta urns like little temples,
Dim-horned sarcophagi surround
        The umbrageous banquet of "this nether-world" —
"Cehen suthi hinthiu":
    Portentious lips reach out to touch us,
As if to say,
    "Welcome. We shall not reproach your stay."
Along the antrum walls,
        Huge, dark-brimmed amphorae;
Alcoves of Cestnal, of Aule, of Vel Partunu;
    Of Larth, chief augur in the city for a while;

Beside him,
   His daughter — Ramtha the sprightly —
      Who died when she was twelve.
Heraldic beasts prance overhead,
     Birds, trees, the festive dancers,
While bands of warrior-statuettes,
        spindly, lofty-crested,
  Muster, in grim ranks, for sacramental war;
And tiny bronze arks of death
   Waft softly over a broad, stellar sea.
Somewhere…a solitary swimmer —
     Ruddy-skinned, supple, nude,
An eye as black as Calabrian wine —
   Sluices downwards through the ocean-shadows:
Slender, mysterious stamen,
   Shrouding the gods about his deep-red shoulders,
Seeking out the hidden Wellspring,
    Proffered Kalyx of the Resurrection.
We end our sojourn thus…
   Ascend into the blanched light of day:
Umbrella-pines around us,
     The scrub-wood, the coastal plains,
A white slab of sea at the far horizon;
     And all is blear and desolate.
The dun hummocks of the dead
  Sleep like ripening melons in the sun.

Keniglekhe Layt

The reproach of His people
Shall He take away
From off all the earth.

Tsiduq Haddin

Winds off the northern steppes
    are husking now
Through musty alleyways
    And tattered fences of the village.
Beneath the eaves,
    Ravens huddle against the night.
I seal the casement shutters…
    …enkindle the lamp upon the table.
The yellow glow embosses
    A samovar,
    A sparkling flask of cherry wine.
I listen to the winds,
    To the drafty silence of my narrow *stubel:*
A mouse
    Scratches at the roof-beams overhead.
I revolve myself;
    My mouth intones the chant —
A song, unending, restless,
    Sputters like a wicker-flame

among the shadows.
"...And it shall come to pass
in the lateness of days...."
For I still hear the ram's-horn
Above those starry tents
And desert twilights.
I have seen the bloom of ancient trees
Upon those stony hillsides —
A beauty yet more breathless
Than prophets' lips,
Hidden, secret, whispering,
The lonely coronation of my soul.
A tasseled shawl,
The many-hued palimpsest,
I deploy around me.
I raise my hands, my eyes...
Torrential winds howl along the gables;
At forest's edge,
The beech trees bend and moan.
On the distant high-road,
A hooded coach, black in the dust of aeons,
Gallops over the storm-dark plains
into the night.

Barcarolle

The slender prow leans forward
      Into silent waters;
The mooring slips away.
      Our loggia upon the trellised isle
Turns and vanishes
  Through cool, morning mists. Before us...
Lagoons beyond lagoons,
     Lavender and organdy in early light,
And beyond the lagoons,
  The salt-marsh, the coastal dunes, the sea.
On the far rivage
     Saplings ripple softly in the breeze.
A heron waits amidst the reeds.
       We watch the vinedressers
Setting out along the distant hills:
     Their flaxen panniers, like doves,
Nod and beck upon the slopes.
     Above the damson forests
In the mountains...
     A solitary cupola...
Almond-white, serene
     Where a wisp of road leads downwards

Through the willow trees —
        And all abides at peace, at peace.
We listen to the oars,
        The rise and dip of oars,
The supple glide of osiers
                And alders at our side.
At lake's marge
        Sails drift on arpeggios of sunlight.
Tidal pools, inlets,
                Over sandy shallows
Flutter homewards,
        Seeking the sea's warm breast
And the warm sea's smile.

Yellow Bird:

Descant on a Popular Theme

Yellow bird,
    Yellow bird:
Downy petal
   in the brightened air;
Through pine-scent
     and lobes of dew,
Pollen-haze
   and willows like a sleepy rain –
Golden burr,
    afloat, afloat,
      …and a child's laughter
Amidst the budding nettles
     of the spring.
Yellow wings,
   Black beak,
     Eyes virid-green:
Aloft, alone
   in the arboreal parquet.
Butterfly,
   Buttercup,
     Bee's flurry ambit –

Sprigs of hollyhock
    and wispy columbine,
Dogwood
        like pink fountains by the stream.
Yellow bird,
            Yellow bird:
Feather-seed
    upon the breeze;
            ...and a child's footprints
In the warm, soft humus
            of the spring.

Ars Antiqua
(organum: triple voice)

Fullness of measure,
bound and winnowed,
welling upwards…
Luke 6:38

ô Child,
Thou hast inherited…
Life…
…Unto all Ages.

❖

ô Oil of Gladness,
ô Spikenard,
ô Emerald Diapason,
ô Child,
Thou hast inherited…
The scarlet-amber oriflamme,
Blazing armature of light –
"Fullness of measure";
ô Child,
Bedecked with galingale,

Currants, dandelions,
Thou hast inherited…
"Bound and winnowed,"
Life…
…Unto all Ages.

❖

ô Seed of Paradise,
ô Cardamom,
ô Luminous Cantilena,
ô Child,
Thou hast inherited…
The multifoliate pericope,
Violet-blue, translucent –
"Fullness of measure";
ô Child,
Bedecked with hyssop,
Carob, coriander,
Thou hast inherited…
"Welling upwards,"
Life…
…Unto all Ages.

❖

ô Child,
Thou hast inherited…
Life…
…Unto all Ages.

Caccia

Behold the scarlet huntsmen!
  The gallant huntsmen!
 Gay damoiselles on tasseled steeds,
Swift, dappled hounds
  among the rhododendrons!
    "Harro! Holloa!"
Bugles blare, the skirl of pipes,
  Glint of spears and jeweled hasps,
Prancing hoofs,
 Embroidered saddles,
Sleeves of sumptuous damascene,
   Disporting through the woodland.
"Arrière! Arrière!"
  "Recover the scent!"
Crumhorns bleat,
 The rattle of quivers, twang of bows;
Brocaded forests
  Redounding with shouts,
   With baying of bounding coursers!
Apricots flame in dark-leaved foliage;
 Crimson gonfalons stream against the sky:
    "Harro! Halloa!"
And the white stag:

Haunches fleet upon the brambly mountains;
Antlers,
　Ruby-studded, *cruciformis*,
　　　Holding up the glorious baldaquin of Heaven,
The amulets of bright-eyed sun
　　　　and dancing moon,
And a billion golden stars.

A Lament: for Gilgamesh of Uruk

(in two voices)

"Have you seen him?
  He has bound the whirlwinds of the sun
And yoked the wide-pronged rivers in his hands.
  He has pitched his tent beyond the mountains
And girt the hills with splendor,
  For the wilderness has flourished in his name.
And the Golden Horns of Uruk
  He has raised above all cities;
He has sheathed its walls with brightness
  And perched its verdant terraces in the sky.
Have you seen him?"

                      "I have seen him.
      He has walked among the Gardens of the Sea.
      He has tasted their pure waters.
      He shall not come again."

"Have you seen him?
  He was the wild bull of the forest,
The wild bull of the plains,
  For he strode the fallow parklands clad in thunder.
Before him danced the lion and the ibex;
  The gazelle and spotted leopard rejoiced to hear his call.

For his arrival was the dawn on river marches,
  Where the sacred ibis rose to glory in his sight;
And his departure was the twilight in the desert,
  Shedding stars like fiery spoors through the night.
Have you seen him?"

                                        "I have seen him.
            He has gone to the Cedar Mountain.
            He has rested in its shade.
            He shall not come again."

"Have you seen him?
  He trod the dusty by-ways of this world.
He only looked before him as he roamed —
  And his heart knelt down inside him.
He mourned upon the ramparts of the city.
  He mourned at the azure gates and by the broad canals.
He mourned in the towered enclaves of the gods,
  For the cup of all his love lay shattered on the stones.
Who, besides him, shall sift the grain aright?
    Who, besides him, shall hew the arrow of his people?
        Who, besides him, shall loose its shaft unto the ages?
Have you seen him?"

                                        "I have seen him.
            He sleeps among the Rainbows.
            His lids are closed forever.
            He shall not come again."

Homage to Aleksandr Solzhenitsyn

Et tu, puer, Propheta Altissimi vocaberis
Canticle of Zacharias

Weep, Holy Child, for the Crown of Kingdom's span
        Has been lost in river's raging flow,
Tears of thunderous war and dire upheaval,
      The tumult and sorrowful agony of the Ages.
Yet, I have seen in your enduring eyes
    Those capacious ploughlands, the dark-green taigas,
Black cypresses at the fringe
      Of snow-capped mountains and tropical seas,
The barren tundras of the north —
        A land most fit, most bountiful
For a realm of grace and valor.
    I have heard in your voice those resonant disclosures
Wherein the tombs of saints and heroes
    Give utterance, wherein the calls of migratory swans
Over lakes and marshes in early spring
       Proclaim that mournful exile, too,
Shall fulfill the days of its tribulation.
    You stand alone, most alone, like a conifer

Amid a grove of leafless, autumn birches,
   Witness to what we no longer even deign to hide:
For our own western asperities —
      Our contempt, our inveterate apostasy —
Have been visited upon your homeland.
    In our irresolute enmity, we think to exorcise
A daimon we ourselves have fashioned,
    A deadly parasite launched upon a spirit
Already too sunk, too burdened,
     By its own multitudinous distempers.
In what nation, in what person,
  When abetted by alien complicity, however disingenuous,
 Do not the darkest inertiae prevail, until...?
O Russia, I see that legendary Wolf
        With glaring garnet eyes
Bounding from your ancient forests,
    His ferocious head, His fine-tipped ears
Surrounded by a radiant nimbus
    Of holiness and justice.
And your dynasts shall fall beneath His stride,
  Though not without admiring His resplendent admonition
Before they perish.
    Upon you has been conferred an awesome humility,
Neither haughtiness nor obsequy,
    But immeasurable composure
  Grounded in untold strength and resolute compassion.
Thus, and only thus,
   You shall have prepared a way before the world.
And you, Holy Child, shall be called

Prophet, eremite, and wandering pilgrim,
Beloved ministrant to all the nations,
Through whom, and in whom, shall be restored
That sacred Diadem,
That hallowed Robe, the Ring, the Seal,
And Kingdom's tolling,
Old-time, long-heard, Peal.

Innsbruck, I Must Leave Thee

(September 9, 1957)

Innsbruck, ich muss dich lassen
ich fahr dahin mein Strassen,
in fremde Land dahin.
Mein Freud ist mir genommen,
die ich nit weiss bekommen,
wo ich im Elend bin.
                    15th Century Folksong

We brought you southward, father,
            Through the Alpine passes
Of the Tyrolean frontier
  To that old, imperial city in the mountains;
And there, among the gray arcades
            and yellow palaces,
  You chose, were chosen, then, to die.
You made no protest.
    It was time: the battered helmet of the age
Slipped from your brow
  And, in your deep-trenched soul,
      An armistice had been proclaimed.
For, at a distance, you had known it all:
  The heritage of battle,
            The reddened eyes of neighbors' children,

[58]

Generations steeped in war
    And crushed, at last, into the vengeful nightmares
Of a maddened despot;
  The bitterness, the anguish, the village shrines;
The empty benches at the *Bierstube*,
    And schoolmates lying frozen on the plains of Russia;
Five hundred years of *raison d'état*,
     Of hegemonies and leagues and armaments,
Burned into the weary hide of Europe.
  Disfigured, too, by the angry moil of history,
That solemn dream of a Middle Kingdom:
      A confederation of ancient peoples —
The Danube and the Rhine —
    Bound in justice, catholicity, and beauty;
A many-tongued choir,
  Raised in unison to Schiller's great Ode:
      "Alle Menschen werden Brüder."
Neither blood nor iron,
  Nor language, nor dominion,
    But only cultivation of the Spirit
As *communitas;*
    And the presence, alone, of that *communitas* —
Multifarious in measure,
    Harmonious in purpose,
      Fruitful in particularity —
As the supreme gift to all the earth.
    And you said that day, echoing von Clausewitz,
"Statecraft is the womb of war;
    Its insidious violence is the bloodshed of the nations."
Then…the sad, soul-wound…
      that vanquished you…!

Did you take it all upon yourself,
Living in a distant country,
     While fine, steep-gabled cities fell into dust,
Shouldering it all,
     In its momentous inscrutability,
   Like one of those sturdy-limbed Bavarian Christs
That D. H. Lawrence saw
     Beside the highland pastures of your native country?
Your soul, father, now, is a chamois
   Upon those white snows and clear-blue mountains,
Free, free,
   From all the world's worry and remorse.
Someday I shall return and see you there,
     Someday shall sing the "grief-turned-splendor"
Of your heart and the heart of Ages.

> *Innsbruck, I must leave thee,*
> *And fare henceforth my ways*
> *To foreign places.*
> *My joyfulness, bereft me,*
> *Comes not to ease my days,*
> *Whom sorrow now embraces.*

Winter in Panchavati

(after the *Ramayana*; in three voices)

"Lordly, these forests in the winter, ô Rama,
    And the Godavari, droning in its deep mountain gorges;
Lordly, these sun-bright uplands and arch-blue skies
    And red jungle blossoms nodding in the breeze;
Lordly, all these tranquil days and starlit, frosty nights,
    When by the warm brazier we blend the fragrant wine —
And we remembered you, Ayodhya, gracious city of flowers,
    Gracious city of the jeweled hills beyond the mountains;
We longed to stand once more at the threshold of your glory."

"Redolent, these sable woodlands in the dawn, ô Sita,
    And the cool, saffron mists from the valleys;
Redolent, these dark winds astir among the bamboo groves,
    And ravines dense with sandalwood and thyme;
Redolent, all these thick-plumed mountains, drenched with dew,
    When in icy torrents we draw the clear ablutions —
And we remembered you, Ayodhya, shining city of garlands,
    Shining city of perfumed gates and golden lattices;
We longed to walk once more in the beauty of your ways."

"Blessed, these shaggy slopes of the foothills, ô Laksmana,
    And the lone mountain elephant browsing in the sun;
Blessed, these pale-brindled deer gathered by mossy pools,
    And the heron bound for the watery plains of the south;
Blessed, all these clouds of evening, brushed with amethyst and gold,
    When in the shadowy forest we awake the sacred flame —
And we remembered you, Ayodhya, jubilant city of bright thrones,
    Jubilant city of proud banners and high pavilions;
We longed to bask once more in the splendor of your days."

Henry the Fowler

The Battle of Riade
Unstrut River, 933 A.D.

What! Grand Carolus dead these many years,
    Who pummeled my wary ancestors into salvation,
Hammering out the battle-shield of his eastern flank;
    And his Empire of the West now but potter's grist
Until Eberhardt, last scion of the Franconian line,
    Should heave the mighty guisarm of authority at me —
I, champion of falconry and feasting in the wood,
    Would marshal all this discord, this rank dissolution:
Bavaria, Lotharingia at war again as usual,
    Burgundy nipping at the heels of tumultuous France,
Saintly Wenzel of the Slavonic Princes
    Slashed by swords on the kirk-porch at Bunzau —
Sole hope of peace traitorously cut down;
    Defenses of the Thuringian marches now burst asunder,
With felonious hordes of fen and grassland
    Like skulls snarling along the hedge of Christendom;
And Gorm the Old, his northern marauders,
    Looting monastic libraries, burning vineyards,
Uprooting all settledness, all civility.
    And I bought reprieve with hostages and gold,
Sought fealty, bonds of friendship
    With dukes and prelates, warlords of the forest,

Taught my Saxon horsemen to deflect
       Sharp barbarian arrows and duplicitous affronts,
Built stockades atop the river-banks,
       Lopped broad-timbered branches across the roads,
Gave heart to my doleful people,
       Girdled all the kingdom in the fullness of its strength.
And they came in the rainy spring,
       Through misty bogs and plains, unknown, unbidden.
We scouted for them by day, by night:
       Envoys scanned the hamlets, the fortress-towns;
Stealthy trackers stalked the lowland swamps,
       And signal fires were kindled on the mountains.
Then, at Riade, we mustered our brave legions,
       Mounting high before us the lofty Whalebone Rood
And Holy Lance of Imperial Constantine.
       Over us, unsteady heavens of storm and sunlight;
Packed battalions sloshed in river shallows,
       Their kirtles soaked and steaming in the morning heat.
The thud, flash of weaponry; shouts, assaults,
       Trumpets honking like wild geese within the bracken,
Sword-hilts slippery with blood and rain
       As thick carnage clotted marshy rivulets and streams,
And mounted spearmen butted, wallowed in the mud.
       Finally, rearing our banners upwards, we invoked
Lord Saba-ôth, Hoarder of Sky's Kingdom,
       From whose stout-thonged, strong-thewed gauntlet
Angelic Mika-El, fierce sparrow-hawk,
       Swooped downwards through thunder-driven clouds,
Bearer of Sun's blazoned baldric,
       Golden-armored, Barb of the Sacred Tempest,
Felled before him the heathen host

That fled to craggy tors, the dense holt and hinterland.
We gave thanks, burying the heroic dead,
        Raising insignia of victory throughout our dominion.
For my progeny, then, to forge a fellowship
        Of tribes and principalities over all the earth,
To resolve the ravenous pagan heart
        With words of covenant, wisdom, and providence,
And within a resourceful world to found
        Habitudes of peace, of learnedness and seclusion
Where justice and mercy may abound,
        Joined together for all ages in regal sanctitude.
To the hawks and steeds, my hearth-friends!
        To the banks and groves of the precipitous Harz!
Let our horns resound above the woodlands!
        We pursue a noble quarry into the valiant dawn!

Terminus: Concedo Nulli

Device of Desiderius Erasmus Roterodamus

The scriptorium has been my domicile.
    From the banks of the Ysel, close by Deventer,
To the Aldine Press in Venice
  Or my chambers in Johannes Froben's house in Basel,
I have beset the libraries of Europe,
   Sending out my *famuli* to search out manuscripts and books —
With these sole purposes:
    To rejuvenate the love of classical antiquity,
To recover *bonae litterae*
 For the repose, the discourse, and the learned piety
Of all mankind, and to approach again
    The sources of Him Who bestowed upon us
Our fragile, inestimable *humanitas*,
  Imparting, in turn, a task almost too onerous to bear,
Though to shun it were ever to devolve
     Into a cataclysm of mendacity and shame.
I have had my friends — Sir Thomas More,
  John Fisher, Cardinal Ximenes of Spain, so many others —
And my adversaries of the hostile camps:
  The popular preachers ranting their officious blasphemies,

Pope Julius and his minions,
    Whom, as was claimed, I had St. Peter brush away
Like malignant horseflies
        From the Gates of Heaven.
    On the other side I fostered, then abjured,
The Monk out of Wittenberg
    Who so savagely decried the surly Roman strumpet,
The selfsame Harlot that Dante saw
      Dandled on squat, imperial knees,
But lowered his eyes,
    Remembering his own lusts, his own excoriate venality.
He cast no stone.
    I, too, have judged; I, too, have come to know
That none but Folly, without impropriety,
        Dare call his brethren fools.
For One, Alone, the Most High,
      May purify the Temple.
And all ceremonies, institutes, and houses
      Are made sound and good unto themselves,
But only soundness and goodness of the heart
    May fathom them and succor them from perpetual decay;
And should they perish,
      The heart shall have no home, no resting place,
No fount to assuage its weary thirst.
    This I have proffered before the ages: wisdom and sanctity —
For sacred thought, sacred erudition,
      At the behest of childlike faith
Shall not fail,
    Though faith shall falter in impoverished intellects,
Minds disinherited,
      Neither *receptores* nor *traditores*

Of such favor, such boundless gifts,
　　Such plenitude of Life in the Legacy of the Spirit.
And yet when He has spoken the final Word,
　"Shall," in His words, "faith still be found on earth?"
Aurelius Augustinus
　　Discerned a City of God in the destinies of men.
Shall our generation then scatter it
　　Among the Kingdoms of the World — soulless, unholy?
The Christian Commonwealth
　　Must be sustained, must be transfigured
Into the fullness of its Being:
　　　Unam, sanctam, catholicam, et apostolicam.
I am the term; I am the boundary stone.
　　I concede, I have conceded, ground to none.
Beyond me naught
　　But arrogance, darkness, and confusion.

A New York Story from the Nineteen-Forties

For that is best; I wol yow nat deceyve.
Chaucer, *The Pardoner's Tale*

On warm summer evenings I used to watch
   The El trains speeding by so closely I could almost touch them
With their electric sparks and strident wheels
   And my mother's Dresden china rattling in the old armoire.
In the street below, neighbors sprawled on doorsteps
  Quarreling and laughing; children played in the dust and heat.
Bars, poolrooms, an ice-cream vendor
   With dented cart and tinkling bells — all did a steady business.
Late delivery trucks drove by.
      And an old bearded rabbi on a wooden bench
Sat apart, a ragged tome cradled upon his knees.
   I, too, sat apart. Within the darkened flat, my father slept,
His newspapers slipping softly from the tattered armchair;
     A burnished cavalry sabre leaned against his shoulder.
My mother sang quietly amid her chores.
  But both of them, even in the sallow twilight of their lives,
Could bequeath all requisite accoutrements of blood:
  A strain of the Viennese, of Budapest, from my father's veins —
Lieutenant once in the Imperial Hussars,
   Right out of an operetta by Johann Strauss or Franz Lehar,

He harried a Balkan peasant or two in his career
  And adorned many a fine parade on the boulevards of the Capital;
Then ended his days in the Bronx,
       Cast off by an Empire gone to seed and dereliction —
Lost all he had: honor, gallantry, the pith of life.
  At my mother's knees, I heard her strange, ancestral songs,
Songs of Ashkenazic minstrels and Gipsy raconteurs
  Who wandered in sometime, somewhere, out of the awesome East.
In her bright, bejeweled heart
    She could weave a rat's nest into a tiara of enchantment.
My years of preening were scrupulous and exact.
    I worked the docks, the great hotels and restaurants,
Absorbing the lore of touring in grand style,
  Of *haute cuisine* and vintage wines, of brandies and aperitifs.
A stint in the Coast Guard inculcated me
    To yachts and yachting saga. I paged Wall Street for a while
That I could ape the capricious ululations of High Finance.
  I studied the museums — the galleries, boutiques, and theaters;
Took up fencing at the "Y", learned equitation
    With New York's "finest", then quit when like my father,
Blue-uniformed and proud, I could ride to stun a crowd.
  At night I perched myself in the very attic of the Met,
Making the world of opera and operatic stars, my own.
      In a dozen ethnic neighborhoods, I deftly collocated
Fragments of a dozen tongues; I traversed the earth itself
    Among the busy street-corners and ghettos of New York.
Then, ready for my entrance in rented evening dress,
    I sported a swarthy moustache, added "Baron" to my name,
And sauntered through the Stork Club as if it were my home,
    Spending in a single evening what I had put aside for months.
Just one appearance, and it worked!

Invitations flooded in, day by day. I only had to get
Where I was going; the rest was supremely "on them."
  Could such opulent missives know the squalor of their destination?
But I gave them what they paid for:
  Lustre, unmatched, amid the unplumbed listlessness of High Society.
I soon concluded marriage with a most beloved woman
    Who understood, *au coeur*, precisely what she was buying into.
Steadfastness and verve and devotion were her emoluments;
      The gifts we bestowed upon each other were justly savored.
For, unlike the rich, I marveled in the realm that I had conquered
    And I showed *them* how to live in it with *Gemütlichkeit*
            In magnificent, old continental style!
I reigned like an emperor at Luchow's;
      I ferried the crowd to Yorktown for Viennese confections,
Frequented Sherry's Bar at the Met, *entr'acte*,
  Attended every opening, paced my great-necked Andalusian stallion
Through the arcades and wooded groves of Central Park,
      Bought imported safari gear at Abercrombie and Fitch,
Had villas in Palm Beach and on the Côte d'Azur.
  My way with those who served was exquisite to the peak
(After all, they know sometimes, infinitely more
      Than those whose studious whims they often tender to;
Yet they can be more arrogant than the rich themselves).
    But what else redeems the all too latent vulgarity of wealth
Than munificence, and beauty, and pruning to perfection
    A knowledge, or a knack, or a precious eccentricity,
That few can cultivate, and that renders in return
        A mirror of Paradise and source of wonder for the world?
A man's life is the story of what he loves;
        And to me such plenteous benefice conferred...!
How could I regret it even for a moment?

Yet why, in my soul's eye, as I lie awake at night,
Do I still watch the El trains on their rusty girders
     Roaring past those poolroom lights and shabby tenements?
Why do I still meditate that ancient man
     Stooped over a worn book on a hot summer's evening?
In only such a desert are voices so resonant and clear?
   I think that I would shuffle off all that's left me now
Of mummery and sham. And I shall wait.
     Life has been so generous. It is so good to live.
I do not think that I shall wait in vain.

Mozart: A Divertimento in F-Minor

Allegro con brio
Andante
Allegro scherzando

I.

Fanfare! Whinny! Flourish of galloping hooves!
  Such sonorous horns over the upland valley!
Spuming manes and horses' crests, like dolphins,
  Cascading by hedgerow and village and copse —
Equipage so gallant, accoutred in blue and gold,
  The raiment of earth so wondrously bright,
As aequiline wings soar high against the sun!
  And the postillion shouts: "Hurry! Hurry!"
Ach, der lieber Wolferl! O amiable fabulist of song!
  Too soon! Too soon! All too soon! —
The carriage tumbles into the haze of dusty roads
  And umber dusk so suddenly above the mountains.

II.

Woodruff, wintergreen, sweet Tokay wine;
  And beyond those marbled terraces,
Fresh prospect of the early spring:

Jonquils and wild mountain ferns
Grow amid the archways and old stone urns.
   At river's bend, a forest minster
Raises knospy spires above the pines.
   Upon the cool tremolo of waters,
Narrow skiffs drift downwards with the current
   Through dappled hollows and shadowy vales,
Where mergansers tune their mournful cry
   And blackthorns bloom beneath the shade.

III.

What joyous bergamasque! *Was für eine Schwärmerei!*
   What refractory filly on the meadow
Feints, sallies, romps throughout the day! —
   While some jocund peasant at the tavern,
His eyes farouche and plump as hazelshells,
   Thumps his foot and puffs upon his bombardon!
And that most punctilious popinjay,
   Glockenspiel a-playing in his fine-harled hands,
Hops gingerly among the woodland glades!
   Meanwhile, behind a gilded choirscreen,
Herr Kapellmeister shakes his impecunious peruke
   And grimly whispers: "Hurry! Hurry!"
Ach, der lieber Wolferl! O amiable fabulist of song!
   Too soon! Too soon! All too soon! —
The ultimate cadenza; the final *"jubilate"*;
   And the pellucid darkness of the grave.

Aeneas Sylvius Piccolomini

The Summit of Monte Cavo
June, 1463

We sit under leafy filbert trees, shelling nuts
And revolving affairs of Church and State.
  Around us, the windy slopes of Monte Cavo
Descend to bright-blue Alban lakes below,
  To hill-forts, and, beyond them, the plains of Latium.
We trace the Tiber's course from Ostia
  To Rome and upwards to the snowy Apennines.
The morning air is calm and luminous.
  We meditate the narrow lip of ancient coast
From Terracina extending northwards
  To Monte Argentario, throned upon the sea.
The pale-blue arch of heaven smiles at us
  And the Signatura, for the day, reposes —
"Amid sweet shade, cool springs, and verdant grass."
  (Bards laggard here could not be spurred by any Muse!)
I walk the narrow goat's path through the glades.
  Ruins of a villa perch on the mountain's edge.
I have the fronds and ivy cleared away
  That we might refresh our somnolent memories.

The ghosts of those old Romans haunt my dreams;
  I would have their spirits up from the dusty tombs,
Though I would also let them sleep for now,
  Nor disturb their monuments and reputation.
What was their own was but uniquely theirs —
  We puff and gesture merely in their borrowed robes,
Our sinews no longer tense with justice.
  For all this beauteous land, this beauteous sea
Harbors armed escorts and contentious fleets.
  The Turkish Lion crouches at the Gates of Europe;
And our kings, like geese, hackle to shore up
  A tawdry pecking line, while waiting for the block.
(They won't be waiting long, as I see it.)
  I would the old Sultan were chief of Christendom,
Should he but dispel the Prophet's slit gaze
  From his otherwise all too sly, capable eyes.
I honor, but will fight, him to the end.
  Meanwhile shall Europe slip into a loathsome mire
Of usury and impoverishment and hate,
  While sorcery prevails, and foul superstition?
States are idols, now, in makeshift temples;
  Banknotes have become their only badge of honor;
The Law of Nations no more binds their hearts.
  Gallic blandishments, complaints of Tuscan envoys,
Venetian traders' dockside invective,
  Sovereigns' quarrels, remonstrances, and bombast
Shower upon my head from day to day.
  The Apostolic Ark itself is foundering.
Cardinal Cusa, Vicar-General,
  Contrives new modes of Church reform, says we must act,
Says the German Princes are rebelling,

[76]

Says that a storm will break from those dim northern skies.
But it's too soon perhaps — perhaps, too late.
   Rebuild a damaged ship at sea and it will sink.
Look at Cusa's efforts in the Tyrol —
   Reforming a single convent landed him in jail,
With old Duke Sigismund, the Profligate,
   Gloating over such an exquisite churchly plum.
Without concord of minds can we reform?
   The Campo Santo, too, must be threshed and winnowed,
Flushing out the Tivoli courtesans
   From the Roman Curia and the Cardinals' beds.
Abbeys, cathedral chapters must be swept
   Where now but asses bray the canonical hours.
And Friars Minor must convert the world
   Before our merchants sell it into enslavement.
This Household of God, Heir of the Ages —
   May it be honed and tuned to all mens' tongues and ears,
Yet altered "not a jot, not a tittle."
   Let true learnedness be the spouse of revelation;
Let beauty adorn our festive worship;
   And let fine craftsmanship abide beneath our roof;
But ask me not to bow my head to fashion
   And divert the career-men from the papal doors.
A scholar's gown often conceals a fool;
   An artist's smock, as well, may mask a shriveled soul.
May Christ be my sole judge in all of this.
   My puppy-bitch, Musetta, almost drowned last week
Splashing wildly in the cloister fishpond.
   I scooped her out; she whimpered, dripping on my lap.
Then the gardener's monkey, lashing free,
   Bit her to the haunch-bone; again, she almost died.

With dark foresight, I bound her bleeding wounds:
   Two mishaps portend a third — unless one repents.
(A dog has no conscience. But what of men?)
   She toppled yesterday from the steeple window
Down into the vineyards. Europe take heed!
   The moment of your apostasy is at hand!
Yet I fear not to thread this needle's eye —
   "Impossible to men, though possible to God."
And my days are lucent with joy and hope.
   The bread and fish are good; the wine is cool and sweet;
Baskets, sevenfold, are filled to the brim.
   The taste of earth consoles us in these latter days,
Made hallowed thus by words, by touch, by breath,
   For this, our generation, and all those to come.

Galileo: A Letter to His Daughter

(Arcetri; March, 1634)

Maria Celeste, your citron jam and candied quinces
    Regale my learned guests; the phial of rosemary-waters
Commends your convent's fine distillery.
    No, my "imprisonment" at home is not as arduous as you think —
After all, the view is superb: Florence, the Duomo,
    The leafy hills beyond the Arno; and I am close to you at last.
I thank you for your offer to recite each week
    Those seven penitential psalms prescribed for me;
What soul could protest an innocence without them?
    Yet I stand, in this case, innocent in my witness to the truth.
For who could disparage such a notion as they hold —
    A whirring glazier's disc, bathed in gulfs of immortal fire:
Earth no more, really, than a mote
    Dead-center, stationary, held in vague sublunary derision
While God's regal wand spins out the planispheres
    Into orbs of searing light and epicycles like webs of glass,
So crystalline and delicate? It's gorgeous to imagine.
    (Though not as gorgeous as what I have actually seen!)

Then am I so audacious as to claim,
        As our Tuscan poet said, mounting the terraces of repentance,
"Si come mostra esperienze ed arte,"
            That God would hurl us like a brazen spear-head
Through immeasurable space,
                Whorl upon whorl redounding all about us,
Ourselves a whorl amid such shaggy planets
    And flaming stars, each arc inscribed so perfectly, so just —
A Universe not hyaline and brittle
            But made of fiery brass and tooled precision;
And all dancing, not to different tunes
            But in one cosmic galliard that measures and ordains
Both the starry lodgements
        And the fall of acorns on hazy autumn afternoons?
We, too, take our part,
        And do not merely gawk like idlers at a country fair.
But be not scandalized at my scruffy waywardness;
            Scholars, not saints, have thus sequestered me.
They, too, — call them what you will:
        Philosophers, men of science, members of esteemed academies —
Coddle their own assemblies of fondly nodding heads
        And skittish tongues. Protest a detail here or there,
Probe a technicality, suggest a "new" interpretation,
    And they'll frown, tilt sagacious eyes, murmur a word or two —
Maybe even land you in a prestigious job!
            But call the entire *modus operandi* into doubt
And you'll end up a-bubbling in a sordid stew.
        They, no less than anyone, will use, if they can,

Engines of relentless power to resolve a squabble
            Or to refurbish a broken pride before the world.
    Yet I hesitate to think what I myself have done
To prejudice or forestall an argument
            Or bludgeon a compeer's intellect before he spoke,
Incurring, thereby, the lash of scorpions' tails.
        Could I not proclaim that the Glorious Lamp of the Universe,
The Parded Sun, aslant upon its golden hinges,
            And all its variant gestures of discovery and prognosis
Have brought upon my head this acrimonious charade?
    As for my adversaries, did not Aristotle muster his precedents
Only to exemplify or confute, never to demonstrate?
            And did Aquinas spar with magisterial hearts and minds
Not to sift, and test, and understand,
        But to expatiate over pompous and mellifluous inconsistencies?
Had the two of them seen the "givens" through my vitreous tube,
    They should have soundly boxed the ears of their unctuous children!
And no mere talk of "saving appearances" for them;
            With loving eyes they would have courteously embraced
The one, unalterable structure of the Universe Itself.
    Yet they knew, as all wisdom must, the limits of presumption.
Protect me, in time, from my own protectors.
                There is no school of thought,
But, without fresh insight and vigorous refinement,
            Distends with age to sophistry and pretension.
And why do those who love the ancients scarcely read them?
        Archimedes, Pythagoras, and Augustine would most gladly share
A cup of wine at my humble board

And wonder who stood without and was battering down my door.
Ah! Maffeo Barberini, how he and I could douse
      A torrid Roman night with goblets of cool Marsala,
Meandering though the gardens of Trinità del Monte
      And babbling all the while about nodes and parallaxes,
Like two old sots
    Rocking back and forth on the lucid horns of a crescent moon!
Now he shuffles along the corridors of the Vatican labyrinth
    Feeling "personally" betrayed, while the Jesuitical gang at court
Meticulously gnaws the innards of his papal ear.
      (The Jesuits know I'm right, and read my books in secret;
Benedictines and Carmelites line up on my side.)
    Meanwhile, the archbishop of Siena does what he can for me;
And Niccolini shunts from Rome to Florence,
      Braving the cold winds of the *tramontana* and hoping to dispel
The mists of malefaction. Barberini mumbles and demurs,
    Then declares for all to hear, "We believe it. We believe it." —
Yet sends no reprieve of that seditious edict he never signed.
    (His own nephew, the Chief-Inquisitor, would not sign it either!)
Maria Celeste, I pray you pray for me;
    And do not worry — in the end, truth will speak in my favor.
The orange trees you asked about are blooming at my window;
      Last week's hail storm did not hurt them in the least.
And "my lady mule" has recovered from her ailment.
      Beneficent old Geppo will load her up with spice-cakes
And bring them to the convent tomorrow afternoon.
      Tell Mother Achilea I have some new sonatas for her organ —
She will like them; and yes, my lute has been repaired.
    And I beg you, in your sick-room duties, be not so overzealous —

Leave something for the novices to do.
    (As if I could tell you that, knowing whose heart you bear!)
And do not yield to dark presentiments —
    You know I could not thrive without your kindly ministrations.
Inscribe your own fine arc, Maria Celeste,
           Through all your days and nights
   In perfect rest and ceaseless energy,
Maria Celeste, Heavenly Star,
        Brightest star in all the firmament for me.

Kyrie: Missa in Aurora

God is an early Riser.
John Donne (*Sermon* on Psalm 90:14)

❖

Lord, have mercy.
R. Christ, have mercy.
Lord, have mercy upon us.

R. LUX FULGEBIT HODIE SUPER NOS.

❖

Kyrie, ô Twilight Breath of Wind out of the Ancient Desert, *eleison*.
R. *Kyrie eleison.*

ô Lone Artisan,
Thou shapest from Night the glowing Helix of Creation, *eleison*.
R. *Kyrie eleison.*
ô Day-Star, Sun of Justice,
Thou arisest in splendor over the Towers of Sion, *eleison*.
R. *Kyrie eleison.*

ô Early Tiller of the Earth,
> Thou sowest in our midst the fecund Seeds of Eternity, *eleison.*
>> **R.** *Kyrie eleison.*

ô Supreme Mysterion,
> Thou shineth forth from the depths of fathomless Wisdom, *eleison.*
>> **R.** *Kyrie eleison.*

Kyrie, ô Fountain of Promise and Chalice of Remembrance, *eleison.*
> **R.** *Kyrie eleison.*

✤

Christe, ô Key of David and Scepter of the House of Israel, *eleison.*
> **R.** *Christe eleison.*

ô Bearer of the Bitter Cup,
> Thou submittest to the Heavy Wine and the Salt-Sea Tears, *eleison.*
>> **R.** *Christe eleison.*

ô Compassionate Wayfarer,
> Thou settest out along the hidden Footpaths of this World, *eleison.*
>> **R.** *Christe eleison.*

ô Wounded Dove,
> Thou art ever borne upon the Sorrowful Rood of Ages, *eleison.*
>> **R.** *Christe eleison.*

ô Perpetual Feast of the Seder,
> Thou rejoicest our spirits at the Banquet of the Kingdom, *eleison.*
>> **R.** *Christe eleison.*

Christe, ô Lion of Judah and Sleeping Lamb of Paradise, *eleison.*
> **R.** *Christe eleison.*

❖

Kyrie, ô Angel of Peace and Mariner of Translucent Oceans, *eleison*.
R. *Kyrie eleison.*

ô Beloved Spouse,
Thou adornest the Nuptial Bed with Violets of Atonement, *eleison*.
R. *Kyrie eleison.*
ô Solace of Nations,
Thou art the Hope and Repose of the Primordial Forests, *eleison*.
R. *Kyrie eleison.*
ô Alpha and Omega,
Thou unravellest the Ageless Vellum of History, *eleison*.
R. *Kyrie eleison.*
ô Trifoliate Rose,
Thou blossomest forever at the edge of boundless Worlds, *eleison*.
R. *Kyrie eleison.*

Kyrie, ô Dew from Mount Horeb, Myrrh of Saba, Coronal of Life, *eleison*.

❖

R. EXSULTA FILIA SION, LAUDA FILIA JERUSALEM.

Lord, have mercy.
R. Christ, have mercy.
Lord, have mercy upon us.

❖

NOTES

p. 3: Epigraph:

> "When I see the lark moving
> With joy his wings against the light
> Who forgets himself and lets himself fall
> On account of the sweetness which enters his heart..."

7: *Berceuse:* a cradle song.

19: "*Ho kakà kakà telôn*": Cf. *Oedipous Tyrannos,* line 1330. The entire line translates as: "*[Apollo] who brings about these my own evil, evil sufferings*"; or, literally, "*[Apollo] who evil, evil fulfills...*"

20: "*The shadowy mountains and the echoing sea*": *Iliad,* I, 157.

21: A canonized saint of the Church, Notker of St. Gall (called "Balbulus") is credited with the invention of the liturgical "sequence." The story of the wolf is apocryphal.

25: Epigraph: "*How good it is and beautiful, for brothers to live in unity.*" The incident described in the poem has been adapted from Guy Sajer, *The Forgotten Soldier* (New York: Harper and Row, 1971).

27: Rome fell to Alaric's Visigoths in 410 A.D., by which time Bordeaux had already succumbed to the Vandals.

33: For the epigraph and for several images in the poem I am indebted to Artin K. Shalian, *David of Sassoun* (Athens: Ohio University Press, 1964). In the poem, Kourkig Jelaly becomes identified with the White Horse of the Apocalypse (Apoc. 19:11).

35: Epigraph: *And the great centaur said: 'They are tyrants*
Who grasped in blood and plunder.
Here they bemoan their pitiless violence;
Here is Alexander...'

The title of the poem is a Middle English variant of
Alexander of Macedonia, indicating its relationship to the
tradition of medieval Alexander romances derived from
works of Pseudo-Callisthenes.

37: For much of the nautical language and the historical back-
ground for this poem, I am indebted to Samuel Eliot
Morison's superb book, *Admiral of the Ocean-Sea* (Boston:
Little, Brown and Co., 1942).

41: For aspects of this poem, especially for the image of the
swimmer, I am indebted to D. H. Lawrence's *Etruscan Places*
(New York: Viking Press, 1957). The Etruscan phrase *Cehen
suthi hinthiu* is translated in the poem by the phrase that
immediately precedes it. See Massimo Pallottino's book,
The Etruscans (Bloomington, London: Indiana Univ. Press,
1975).

43: *Keniglekhe Layt:* "kingly people." *Tsiduq Haddin:* the name
of the Hebrew Burial Service, which translates as "righteous
judgment." *Stubel:* room.

43: *Barcarolle:* Venetian boat song.

51: *Caccia:* an early Italian Renaissance hunting song, here inter-
woven with medieval French motifs.

53: Helpful for the construction of this poem were S. N. Kramer's
Gilgamesh translations in James B. Pritchard, *Ancient Near
Eastern Texts Relating to the Old Testament* (Princeton, N.J.:
Princeton Univ. Press, 1955).

56: A Russian legend of a Divine Wolf can be found in Ivan Bunin, *Dark Avenues and Other Stories* (Westport, Conn.: Hyperion Press, 1977).

60: The D. H. Lawrence allusion is to his essay "The Crucifix Across the Mountains" in *Twilight in Italy* (New York: The Viking Press, 1958). *Grief-turned-splendor:* "All grief in time shall turn to splendor for posterity. All heirs shall wear past destinies as an adornment": Rainer Maria Rilke, *Notebooks*, October 4, 1900.

63: Henry the Fowler was a Saxon king and founder of the Holy Roman Empire. He died in a hunting accident in the Harz Mountains of Germany soon after his victory at Riade.

66: *Terminus: Concedo Nulli:* "[I am the] limit: I yield to none."

79: Sister Maria Celeste, a member of the Poor Clare convent of St. Matthew near Florence, was the eldest daughter of Galileo. She died on April 1, 1634, at the age of thirty-three. Consult the intriguing study by Mary Allan-Olney, *The Private Life of Galileo* (Philadelphia, 1869). The quotation from Dante is drawn from *Purgatorio*, 15, 21 and means: "As experience and art demonstrate."

80: Aeneas Sylvius Piccolomini was Pope Pius II, a renowned Humanist scholar of his time. This poem is based on the *Memoirs of a Renaissance Pope: The Commentaries of Pius II* (New York: Capricorn, 1962).

85: This poem combines features of traditional Advent antiphons with the medieval troped kyrie, as exemplified in *The Sarum Missal* (Oxford: Clarendon Press, 1916) and *The Winchester Troper* (London: W. H. Frere, 1894). Latin passages have been added from the Introitus and Communio of the Missa in Aurora (Christmas Mass of the Dawn).

Johann M. Moser, Ph.D.

Poet Johann M. Moser lives with his family in an eighteenth-century cottage surrounded by fields and woods overlooking Squam Lake, New Hampshire, with a magnificent view of the White Mountains.

Moser's father, August, a young German pediatrician, opposed the Nazis and had to flee his native Garmisch-Partenkirchen just before World War II broke out. August came in exile to the United States, where Johann, the second of his eleven children, was born.

Although Moser's mother was born in the United States, she had a cosmopolitan influence on Johann, for she spent much of her lifetime abroad.

Johann Moser himself lived and received his early education in New York City, but has lived in many other parts of the United States and in Paris, and has traveled extensively in Europe.

As an undergraduate at Dartmouth College in New Hampshire, Moser combined his interests in literature, language, and ideas by studying poetry with Richard Eberhart while taking a degree in philosophy.

Moser received his doctorate in Comparative Literature from the Catholic University of America in 1970. He has also attended classes in Chinese literature at Stanford and literary prosody at Harvard.

Johann Moser sees the purpose of poetic composition to be the creation of finely-crafted, beautiful artifacts of language, each with an integral, self-contained, and cohesive structure. In medieval terms, he seeks to achieve in each of his poems a *splendor formae* — a radiance of formal unity.

As a poet, he feels closest to Milton and other seventeenth century poets. Among modern writers, he has most intensively assimilated the work of Ezra Pound and Rainer Maria Rilke.

The wisdom gained from Johann Moser's lifelong studies of other ages and cultures permeates his poetry. His first published volume, *Most Ancient of All Splendors*, reflects a multitude of literary traditions extending through the Middle 'Ages and Græco-Roman Antiquity to include Ancient Near Eastern, classical Chinese, and even Sanskrit models.

Yet Moser places particularly strong emphasis on the Christian (and especially Catholic) elements in our Western intellectual and artistic heritage — because of the energy and colorfulness of this tradition, its inherent religious and metaphysical richness, and its moral authenticity.

In addition to writing poetry, Moser teaches literature at St. Anselm College in New Hampshire.